The Gist Of It

Youri Young

Presentation by *BookLeaf Publishing*

Web: www.bookleafpub.com

E-mail: info@bookleafpub.com

ISBN: 9789357615440

First edition 2022

*To the one who pushed through it, survived,
and learned to find beauty in damn near
everything - I love you*

ACKNOWLEDGEMENT

There have been so many peers, teachers, friends, and mentors that have encouraged me to gather my work into a collection. Without them I would not be the writer I am today and I will be forever grateful for the friendly words and the nudges in the right direction. Thank you!

Cover art created and painted by
Ameera Al-Maksosi.

PREFACE

Brace yourself. Some of these pieces will highlight and attack traumas that have shaped the person that Youri is today. This is by no means in attempt to trigger anyone but the possibility of doing so is real. Take what you can use to improve your situation, switch your perspective, open a new mindset. If nothing else is to be taken from this book it is this: you don't need to have it figured out right now, be present, be you.

Queen of the Roses

You with all of your elegant beauty, lips more red than rubies, whose seemingly solitaire duty is to glisten and gleam, somewhere between the dazzling stars and the dancing of sunlight that bounces off streams. Yes, you. Why do you pain me so? You must know by now that I will remain undaunted, unpained, and unhaunted by whatever lies behind or beneath where your bristles grow. So show me your endless reserves of strength you preserve in an armoire of treasures and riches. Show me your mental capacity that dares the audacity to create with both hammer and stitches your armor and sword, not for fighting or war, rather for fending off judgemental bitches, who chase nothing more than your alluring appearance. This grievance displeases those who have learned that they ought to yearn to earn your respect and acquaintance. Should they not adore you? Queen of the Roses. Should they not adorn you with copious stories of your immortal glories and focus their every energy on your heavenly reverie? Should they not implore you to bequeath and bestow a fragment of your endless talent though they be beneath and below the worth of the dust of your feet? Like veins of magma that flow under the surface of skin that covers our Earth Mother. They boil with rage. And though they roar as the thunder when the sky unloads the rain, you thrive and retain your limitless luster. And muster the strength to hold your head high and strike like the lightning, not with weapon or force, but with frightening beauty and inexorable grace. Your visage shines bright as though dew drops embellish your face. Stand proud in the place where you've so long been shackled, to the same soil that brought budding new life from your roots. Until they deduce that they can reduce you of worth as it suits them. They cut you down and displace you, decrown and disgrace you. In an ornate and intricate vase they display your truncated, intimate carcass so openly. Hopelessly overlooking your inborn potential for greatness, they gaze at your beauty with envy and scorn. Yet, you do not mourn their open disdain. You know just as sure as the clouds come with their rain and the sun rises with morn, as certain as harvest brings grain, barley, or corn, no matter what ill will their desire imposes you are Queen of the Roses. You were born wild, beautiful, sought after and free. So let them be warned, this is written and sworn: every woman is a rose and every rose has its thorns.

Smile

He asked her

"How can you still smile after all you've been through?"

She answered with that same smile that had seen so much

"Because, I am not what I have been through, and my smile is what has got me here."

Ready Your Hands

Ready your hands.

I grew up in a bilingual home. And let's see if
you can spot the difference of tone in these two
phrases. Pa renmen ou. Pare men ou. The first
means I don't like you. The second means ready
your hands. But they may as well have been the
same. It never took long for the lump in my
throat to form when I would hear these words. A
reaction well outside of my control but one I had
to learn to mask. They would never ask. Only
tell. Only spell out exactly how they planned to
hurt you and quite literally add insult to injury
with tongues of fire that whipped harder than the
belt ever could. Words broke less bones than the
broomstick but shattered confidence instead. If a
child's self image is broken in a next door
apartment and the neighbors are right there,
close enough to hear it, does it make a sound?
Or is it drowned out by the fear and the pleading
through the tears and the bleeding of a child
beaten for hours while cowering curled on the
floor, not knowing when they'll be allowed to
crawl their battered body back to bed so they can
recite the lies they would tell to their friends

about their new bruises and scars. Was it so hard to see what was happening? Could no one understand the flinch of fear when my fathers hand would come near me for any reason whatsoever? Ready your hands. So I can use mine to make yours swell with pain. Ready your hands. So I can have somewhere to aim. Ready your hands. So I can transfer my anger, stress from my bad days, my sorrow from sad days, and let your little hands hold all of it for me.

Steady your hands.

Don't lose your grip. Physically, mentally. Never let slip what little control you still have. Never react out of anger, worry, or fear. Never let anyone get near to this version of you that you've hidden and guarded. It hurt. It took time. But you finally discarded the pain you've held onto by digging and internally trapping the load. Now the emotions that come with that must never be shown. Steady your hands. No trembling or tears from the things that have hurt you. Steady your hands. Do not reach them back out towards those that desert you. Steady your hands. They'll expect you to buckle. They'll expect you to break. But despite all the weight that you levy, learn that no matter how heavy your hands get you cannot let go.

Heavy your hands.

Perfect it all. From schoolwork and friendships to pass-times and jobs. Be the best. And not just the best that you can be. BE THE BEST. Test your limits again and again. Stretch yourself thin if you have to. If somebody asks you for this, that, or the other, bring them and then somes, an and one, and extra just to be sure. Do not expect a return, a thank you, or acknowledgment at any level. Never settle for being average or taking the same route that others would. They can be good. You will be better. You will endeavor to be massive even among giants. Like Atlas of old you will hold the two poles of this world between your hands. And then add the moon to the load. Heavy your hands. Do more and be more. Heavy your hands. Hold the weight of the world, no matter how unyielding and massive, until it feels fleeting and passive and you're ready to add to the burden. Heavy your hands. But do not let them see the struggle and strain behind the closed curtain. And above all, do not let them know how deadly your hands can be.

Deadly your hands.

You are not without fault. You have no stone to cast and the glass walls wherein you stand could not take that pressure anyway. The messages these hands have typed and sent have left others in speechless ruin. You are no saint here. You have no place here. Among the people you have used these deadly hands to hurt. Among the people who saw worth in your smile and light in your soul. Do not feign seat at their table or spot in their home. Deadly your hands have been and deadly do they remain. Chained to a cycle of sin and pain that's self-inflicted. And though you've prayed and wished it to be better with deadly hands grasped together in gesture of humility, there can't really be a change until you release what's dead and heavy, learn to finally steady and ready your fucking hands.

Coffee Stains

I am a seed, I suppose. The chemicals that compose me will decompose and bleed my life force into the ground. My roots reach down, spread out, and surround me in a fortress of solitude. Let the earth, which resides in the depth of my iris, be imbued with the virus of piety. The paradox lies in the sense that in this unstable and uncertain society we leave no room for dubiety. So cling to me. I am a deity. I will hold you tighter than the grip of addiction from the nicotine in the cigarette sticks I slip between my rose red lips. While like Atlas of old I spin on my axis and hold the two poles of this realm in calloused rough palms, and direct you to follow the stars as you sail across my sun-kissed skin and find there in, within this wrinkle of time we call life, my reason for living eternally. I am diurnally hoping my internal stains are from coffee not sin. I am akin with the nature of time and its flow, but, for reasons unknown, I'm not bound by it. I stem from a place that exists before the beginning. Yesterday I was, I am, and will be. Today I am me. Tomorrow the world will keep spinning and my garden will bloom. Roses entomb my core as their thorns draw out

of me a river of tears. So, cheers with a coffee
mug that will spill down its side to restain the
inside of me. In hindsight my open third eye
could see that time and me are cognate. We are
intimate. I am infinite.

Perspective

The silver linings of cloud 9 once held a radiant hue. When happiness went 'round like time, so splendid were the views. Majestic as it may appear, the sunset mocks with all its beauty. The far reaching dichotomy of comfort and of cruelty. Crepuscular creeps now my soul, and moons know well my tears. Darkness begetting darkness, sadness begetting fear. I wither where the woes will wilt and bloom where sorrows sprout. Where tears once fell my blood now spills as happiness runs out. In silence sink the memory of joys I dared imagine. And clouds once gray grow colder still and somehow ever blacken. Rain, now snow, falls dark as ash upon my sullied crown. And stumbling, I search for any lining on the ground. Bitter be the fallen, depressed are the depraved. While lifeless me breathes sighs of grief within a living grave. One single ray of sunshine reflected by the moon. In tandem falls with ashen snow to rest upon my tomb. It reads, "Here lies his smile and sorrow, here lies his love and pain. Words understood tomorrow are words written in vain."

The silver linings of cloud nine all hold a radiant
hue. Sending happiness around like time, with
such celestial views. Majestic shines the sunrise,
the sunset falls with beauty. Look up, allow the
sunlight to carry out its duty. Though
crepuscular may creep the soul, the moon will
know no tears. Darkness gives way to light
again, hope erases fear. Where withered we,
wallowed in grief, watch closely as we bloom.
To spring from death, post final breath, our joys
conquer the tomb. The storm clouds have their
beauty too, and purpose all the same. For winter
yields to darkened skies as springtime brings the
rain. The heavens weep to part with snow but
welcome in new life. The same for we see as we
grow we learn from toils and strife. Bitter be the
hardships that befall the dear depraved. Sour be
life's lemons, til we make them lemonade. That
golden ray of sunshine, that pillar beam of
moon, that smile, that friend, that memory, that
sappy summer tune;
Find joy where others do not search
Love, learn, and freely give.
You are here right now, alive
So do not forget to live.

The Willow

Resting beneath the willow
And the cheerful life of spring
When flowers bud
And strangers love
And birds begin to sing

Hearing the sea waves crashing
Feeling the warm, soft sand
And asked to choose
Between this and you
I'd always take your hand

I'm ashamed that I have not yet found a way to
suitably articulate how I feel about you. I could
try to tell you that it's hard for me to breathe
without you. That my heartbeat quickens every
time I think about you. That I've told myself that
I have to fess up, but every time that I'm about
to, I get too worried I'll mess up and make a fool
of myself. So I stay quiet and decide to keep my
feelings locked inside and try to hide my love
away. And in the day it isn't hard at all. But
when night falls and I drift off to sleep with my
head upon my pillow I dream of

Resting beneath the willow
And the summer's gentle breeze
Of butterflies
And waterfalls
On hikes I traipse with ease

Hearing the sea waves crashing
Feeling the warm, soft sand
And asked to choose
Between this and you
I'd always take your hand

I don't know how to tell you that your smile can
make my day. Outweigh all the negativity that
hangs over me like masses of lightning charged
gray storm clouds ready to pour on my
unsuspecting parade. From across a crowded
room your smile feels like a warm embrace as if
you've laced your arms around me in an effort to
revive desires to waltz out in the rain. This
warmth seems to billow from inside me. Your
smile reminds me of

Resting beneath the willow
And the endless charm of fall
Amber leaves
And colored trees
And really most of all

Hearing the sea waves crashing
Feeling the warm, soft sand
And asked to choose
Between this and you
I'd always take your hand

One day soon I'll hopefully find the perfect
words that can describe how you are, if but in
my eyes, the most beautiful soul that this world
has ever known. How when I'm with you I feel
at home. How you make me believe that I'm
worthy of love when no one else that I've ever
met could. And should you ever ask me for what
I so longingly dream as I gaze out the window. I
will tell you I'm wishing for

You by my side in the shade of the willow
In winter, in summer, in autumn, in spring
Walks through the park near a pond filled with
minnow
Enjoying the songs of the birds as they sing

The smell of the salt in the ocean before us
As we sit on a blanket enjoying the view
Your hand in my own as the waves strike their
chorus
My love, I have always been wishing for you

Yin Yang

Push and pull, hot and cold, ebb and flow, to and fro, I've learned that opposites aren't so much so, they're much more alike than they let on. It's an astonishing phenomenon. What would one be without its antithesis? What is guilt without innocence? What is the end without the genesis? And the list goes on and on. Arrival without exodus? Alien without indigineous? Simple without rigorous? You will uncover more and more the longer this is pondered on. Mountain without precipice? Belief without incredulous? Incompetence without specialists? See, they all share a common bond. A foundation without an edifice? A labyrinth without Daedalus? Débutant without emeritus? Giving without ungenerous? In the quiet is found the resonance that speaks volumes. The muses in their ballrooms encourage us to dance. The stance and steps of which are in perfect pitch and unity with the trance of standing still. How transient the thrill of comforts made to last forever. How ambient the chill of slumber made to never sever. See death to me is simply living without sign of life continued still restrained to bone and sinew. Find within you strength, purpose, joy, and depth. Life and death are opposites and opposites attract; which would mean we have to lose our life before we ever get it back. If life's a one way ticket that can only lead to death? Does death then offer up new life after our final breath? The harmony is so intricate it may as well all be the same. The balance is so delicate between all yin and yang. What is love then without hate? What is master without slave? What holds me captive to my innate desire to be seen as someone great? But also to expire soon and retire early to my grave? The moon and ocean push and pull my soul in separate ways. And agony becomes my peace. I find solace in the pain. Tranquility will purge me of hostility in my veins. Harmony will plant within me the ability to remain open to the change and versatility of this realm. The ability to relinquish control and let the cosmos take the helm. Allow yin and yang to overwhelm me completely. Allow yin and yang to compel me and complete me.

Captain of the Clouds

The sun, celestial in its glory knows not story that differs from a path that never swerves and somewhere in his core he yearns to be released. To travel freely and grace other atmospheres with life giving warmth and light. Caliginous, the moon some nights knows only halves of faces, rolling phases through a cycle once again whose end draws never nearer. The more I peer into this mirror of existential self reflection the more I fear a resurrection to the repetition and the known. A life renewed, as is, would be so prone to mundane monotony. Half assed mediocrity that begs the push of pent up potential. But we were taught to be more stencil than man, corralled by commands that sounded a lot like suggestions to 'color within the lines'; which is simply to trace the musings of somebody else's mind. How are we to think when we are told time and time again that history repeats. And yet they say the grandiose feats of the Martin's and the Park's are not meant to be repeated by the likes of me. They tell us we were never made to be kings and set their roses on display. Contained by vase and title they have made us tame and bridled power they should have never hoped to control. And then console us with the calculated lie that you can be anything you set your mind to. So long as you don't realize that you've been lied to and pick the career they've pushed you towards with tests of aptitude, school grades, and systemic regulations. This subtle degradation happens slowly over time. They pull at our minds until we can recite their half truths from memory as if we penned the lines ourselves. But to hell with that. To hell with anything that's ever held me back and that includes myself. I've been through the darkness and made it out the other side without anybody's help. I've learned truths about this world that left me shell shocked and changed my entire perception on life. So to anyone who's ever questioned why I choose to write here it is: Everyday I'm gifted life without a promise of tomorrow. Time is borrowed and I don't have enough of it to figure out where the hell it's loaned from, so I refuse to be some loathsome dreamer who would excuse his talent as if the talons beneath these eagle wings I soar with weren't made for winning wars with. I won't be silenced by a system that makes the victim suffer all the more only to profit from their pain. I've gained my stripes and though I may not have the ancestral scars as proof, the stars and moon bore witness to my struggle. The blood on these black knuckles has never been my own. I have been fighting to make this body home since the minute I stepped inside of it. The utter strength and size of it has never felt like it provided it's full intensity so I found hope in mentally crafting remedies that often had the tendency to exit me as melodies that took on a complexity of their own. Eventually my words became a specialty, the pen and pad my weaponry, and this skill that I will hone could dismantle a hegemony, so if you step to me you better watch your tone. I'm not known for being violent.

But when they say the pen is mightier than the sword,
just know that means you can't afford to throw words
out in a careless manner. Even for those who attempt
to oppose me I am here to be planner, life coach, and
helpful adviser. So just know if you want it like that,
I've been a fighter since diapers. Before you can hope
to decipher the cypher I'll have you in scope like the
eye of the tiger. No Rocky but I'll have your back on
the ropes like Mike Tyson, the biter. Between the
incisors goes all of the jokes 'bout "he's just a writer"
as you're getting choked cuz my jaw at your throat
keeps biting down tighter. Your eyes open wider,
your soul starts to float, your body feels lighter, and
with use of these quotes, the gold on the Icarus wings
that I tote, I'll show you why I have been labeled a
GOAT since I picked up a notepad and called myself
a writer. The sun. Though celestial in its glory pales
in comparison to the story of my sails that caught the
wind to make me captain of the clouds. So as you
shoot for the stars, I'll sail on Milky Ways, holding
jesting conversations with whatever face the moons
will show. I, too, know the feeling of concealing who
I really am and waning as the days roll by. But now
soaring endless sky as my foundation, I fly without
course or formation of a plan that shackles me to any
hand that I am dealt. Call my bluff if you don't
believe me but the chips will always fall to me
because I'm free to lay whatever card that I so
choose. I am dealer of this destiny. It is mine and
mine alone. I fully own all that is meant for me and
lay my claim by making known that I'll be taking
everything. If I can't be king of anything I'll be the

prince of all instead. The ball of thread that weaves
my tapestry is actually the summary of agonies
derived from countless travesties I avidly converted
into mastery of both self and situation. So I let
baffled be those who think mortality is my final
destination. With each piece that I pen I am reborne
again to live lifetimes in the hearts where my words
will find home. Each stanza of poem is reincarnation
of flesh and of bone, of interpretations of me that will
live without end. I am sun, I am moon, I am me still
the same, I speak my story and name through the ink
of my pen.

To You

If I had the chance to meet you. To seat you at my table, offer you a drink, and speak to the things I wish someone had told me when I was young. Not so much to teach you, but maybe only see to it you might avoid some of the things that I have done. Give you pointers on how to overcome the challenges this life will throw your way. Help you learn things no one taught me until it was just about too late. Help you rewrite your own fate. Like if Shakespeare got to write the script after the critics got to sit and review his latest play. We could inkblot every day in which I already know the clouds are dark and dreary. Make sunshine, and ocean breezes, starry nights, where motion ceases and time learns to stand still. The world could exist as you believe it, as if the cosmos knew to bend to your grand will. Help you not to make mountains out of small inconveniences, but rather turn seemingly big problems into minuscule anthills. Help you to remain tranquil. And when the muses start to play their tunes in hopes that you staunchly refuse that you refuse yourself the urge to be fluid free and loose i would make use of the chance to teach you how to dance till you

assumed that Cupid slipped a drop or two of
potion right into the juice that you had chosen to
open, not knowing how potent a drug love could
be until you were so happily love drunk on
living that you forgot, unlike time, how to stand
still, and before you knew it you'd lost track of
the moments that stopped, popped cork after
cork off each bottle of life until
 the world spun around so fast that even when
your half full glass turned upside down you
found out that it still can't spill. Imagine the
thrill of knowing what options, decisions,
choices, words, actions, mindsets, mannerisms,
and behaviors would favor your every turn.
Imagine knowing which path you should take
every time that you wake to ensure you a quick,
safe return. Imagine getting to learn that a fire is
hot without getting burned. Imagine being able
to preemptively discern every cause for concern
in every event you would ever be faced with.
Imagine knowing every surprise that life had
been storing. Honestly, I really don't know if I
could picture anything as pointless or boring.
Because what would life be without uncertainty
and doubt? What would sunshine feel like if it
was never hidden by clouds? What wonders
would an ocean really hold if we were not
accustomed to dry ground? What thrill is left in
flying if we had never been held down? No, if I

had the chance to meet me, if my path was spun round, and I was sat down with my younger self, I think I would tell me this: life is full of twists and turns, but opposition exists to help us learn what living really is. Your comfort zone will kill you slowly, ever tightening binding chains. Don't be afraid of what lies beyond your understanding, don't shy away from change. What you already know can't help you grow, and you can always rearrange the seeds you sow because nothing stays the same forever and though what is new often seems strange, in practically every endeavor it's necessary to try, to fail, to fall, and then get up and try again. Because you're doing alright. Believe it or not, everyone, you included, is allowed to make mistakes. Everyone at some point has to slam on their brakes, to evade total disaster then do a quick double take when they realize the pedals they pushed only made them speed faster towards what they tried to avoid. And we can either choose to be annoyed at these humanoid bodies and minds that allow imperfections, wallow in anguished abjection, persist in dark disconnection from former projections of happier days; or we can allow these misfortunes to spark introspection that move us towards warmer directions and better our ways. We are masters of fate. Writers of destiny. So, when trial

and tribulation come to kick in the door, do not
deplore poor decisions made until now. We will
stumble, get up, and choose to be better, we
won't throw in the towel until we've conquered
adversity, made an absolute mockery of any
paltry attempt meant to condemn or fumbling
foe sent to overwhelm us in sorrows and
suffering. We will welcome the hardships
because more often than not it's the terribly hard
shit that can truly unearth the pure gold that your
oversized heart is actually composed of. So
maybe now in this moment you feel rather
disposed of, or the people you thought you were
most close to, who were supposed to devote
some of their efforts to love and support you,
chose to forgo the quo and for reasons unknown
now decide to oppose you. Perhaps in an attempt
to provoke you to explode soon they hoped to
force you to erode and decompose through their
efforts to promote a more morose you. They've
engrossed you in their gross views and now
choose to attempt to control you all in hopes
you'd feel alone. Please remember that they're
wrong. Whether or not you believe you've got a
pissing pot or spot to squat, do not permit the
thought to taut knot itself where it ought not to
be. The decisions you've made have led you
perfectly to this moment in time. And though the
path may be rocky the climb is worth all the

effort. One day you will be able to look back and treasure each moment that created the landscape of your life. Each valley and peak, each low and each high. You will stand on the precipice of your own mountainside, breathe deeply, and gaze at what you will then realize is the splendid summation of the spirited fight you put up when it seemed that your entire world had caved in. You will smile, all because way back when you did not lose sight of your own glorious light, and you'll be forced to acknowledge that you've learned, that you've grown, that the potential you've shown your whole life became a force to be reckoned with, that you will not back down or give up no matter what you are threatened with. And when met with difficulty or somber misfortune, you'll respond precipitately having learned the importance of prolificacy that is most commonly forged in magnificently choosing not to abort when the comforts you seek that had not long before been traditionally all that you'd been absorbed in, unexpectedly become moot, unimportant. You will come out of this right where you need to be. So believe in yourself even if you don't believe me. Make something of your talents and push past pain, fear, and self doubt, what you need to be successful has been within you all along. Your capabilities are infinite and you are strong. Your

speech is articulate and you belong. Write freely.
Breathe easy. Be cheesy. Love deeply. Even if
it's only briefly. Because no one is here for long.
Before you know it, you'll be gone. So live life
like you were dying because each breath brings
death one half step closer. We're all tall enough
to ride this rollercoaster we call life so square up
your shoulders and lift up your hands. Scream as
loud as you can. Make each moment
worthwhile. Remember to smile. Smile until you
forget that you have to remember. Be kind. Treat
everyone as though they were a member of your
family tree, the one that you have planted,
because remember you sow the seeds and
granted blood makes you related, but love is
what makes you family. And even if you don't
end up being all that you have planned to be; I'll
love you all the same because you are what
made me, me. It's your time, it always has been,
so go on and take your shot. And when you find
yourself in my spot, sitting with our younger
self, make sure to tell us anything that you may
think that I forgot.

What If

What if you were the difference between sorrow and smile? The center of yesterday, now, tomorrow, and a little while? In the middle I'll discover who it is I really am. The identity of these hands is complex when each extremity gets blessed with extra context to make convex and bend the object of who we really are. Maybe ideas and concepts conceived by those who believe they know us better than we do are more see through than how we choose to portray ourselves. Yet still, the world and its status quo can help us grow to find who we are and know who it is we want to be. What if our insecurities were formed just to make sure that we don't conform or buckle under pressure? What if the looking glass that we assume that people pass their gaze through was more prism than scope? So that we could take on multiple shapes, be shoulder to lean on, sunlight or stars, Jupiter, Mars, or simply a beacon of hope with a smile and a kind word. What if all that shines wasn't gold, but silver instead? What if we choose now to embed the idea that we are only human? These hands we hold are as complex as our identities. And What If that's how it was meant to be? No two fingerprints the same so we can leave our own mark on history. Different scars and different stories, different paths all full of mystery and purpose. Burning heart to serve as furnace to the hearth that houses our eternal soul. What if forever comes today? And I believe it does. Because yesterday remains what was and tomorrow never gets here. The sorrows that beget fear are often traumas that resurface. And though some are only skin deep we then seek to play epidermic Tetris with our broken pieces. What if the thesis, purpose, and meaning of life are all one and the same or at least somewhat aligned? What if it's just about enjoying the passing of time? Dancing through rhymes and rhythms, owning respective isms, honing perspective prisms, that is to say learning to read between the lines but also see the bigger picture. What if we understood that love runs thicker than blood, and loyalty and trust run thicker still? What if we cried over the milk we spill because it's okay to feel emotion? Running through the motions equals movement but that's not the same as progress. What if we learned to trust the process of just letting go? Letting show our hurt and imperfections. What if through guided self reflection we faced the demons we've been running from to save ourselves becoming some and finally find connections?

What if the universe was infinite and ever
expanding in every direction? Where would the
middle be? It would mean that you and me stand
always at the center of all things that are. The
center of sun, moon, planet and stars. The center
of hearts and homes, thoughts and poems. We
are the unknown and the limitless. We can
outgrow what inhibits us by learning to
understand our potential. What if we really are
that special? Through the prism of the looking
glass we find the concave bigger picture. We
find the wealth that makes us so much richer
than money ever could. We find the good in life,
the pure of heart, what's meant for us, what's
meant to be. And we what if we finally decided
to take it?

Love Grief

Maybe grief is love's way of reminding us that we're still capable of feeling. Showing us we're healing although painful be the process. Maybe sometimes progress slows because it knows that speed is not a one fits all solution. Maybe confusion in the chaos is the only way we cope. Maybe hope's the drug that kills you slowly with promises of a tomorrow that you will never see because you will forever be resigned to live today. Maybe it's designed to be this way so we can stay afloat amidst the wreckage of a world that tries to drown us. Maybe grief is love disguised, maybe pain is simply feeling but sometimes heavily intensified. Maybe pride is innate preservation, fear; survival's hesitation, and chaos the only true order of a divine that does not exist. Maybe this is the truth, and the truth is simply love. Maybe love is the chaos and the chaos is simply us.

Or maybe not.

Falling Again

Often I feel like I watch my life from another's
point of view
Before my own, I put others' needs, desires, and
often feelings too
And though I've grown and learned from past
mistakes it seems that fate wants me to see that
history repeats
But I have learned.
Defeat is not disaster, anymore
Though I'll get burned, and it will always hurt to
be ignored
I'll keep knocking on that door
Until I find someone who loves me in a way that
I deserve
I know my worth
And I won't doubt me anymore
As I rack my brain, I realize I've been this way
for as long as I recall
Ready to give and gain so much, but terrified to
lose it all
Because I know just where my love is now and
remember where it's been
And every time I choose to let it out, it's broken
me within

Excuse my doubts, my walls, my guards and
such it's all that I can do
To keep my fragile heart from falling hopelessly
in love with you

Looking For Love

I've heard it said that we accept the love we think we deserve. Since I first understood this, this phrase has only served to unnerve me. What love am I worthy of? Love has always been my sort of achilles heel. Which is more unideal than you might assume. When I fall, I'm consumed, I fall hard and for real. Any attempt to repeal or steele up my emotions tends only to seal my fate. I'm not sure how I feel. I'm not sure if real love is true or if true love is real. I believe that we try to conceal our hope that love is all that it's said to be. Which only perfectly reveals how we cling to love so tenderly. I want love like the elderly. A love that has grown for the majority of a century. We could leave behind a legacy. Passed down through our pedigree of exemplary ancestry. I want to be able to adore someone though I'm not all there mentally. And when memory starts fading and energy starts failing me I want to be sure that I loved someone splendidly. And age might inch me towards a grave quite rapidly, but it will all be ok, no that won't bother me, because I would know I loved in full. I want to love like a fool that's in too deep. Be swept up off my feet by a sudden rush

of infatuation. My innate sense of self
preservation stripped from me momentarily as I
let down my guard. Discard the walls around the
graveyard of my heart temporarily to make room
for another lover's unfamiliar touch of a
treasured memoir marred. I want to love new
and fresh, in the honeymoon phase, where we
can do no wrong. For that month or two we
simply belong to each other because that's just
what the fates have planned out. Let the
alignment of the planets map out the trajectory
of this crash course they've set for me. Because
inevitably we'll run out of things to talk about.
The spark will burn out and we'll ghost each
other. And it's no hard feelings toward the other,
that's just the way of life, love, and lust. They
are all by products of one another. I want to trust
someone enough to love them. I'm not dumb
though, if I could I would numb my heart in
preparation because I know love will hurt. But I
hope that I find someone that makes the pain
worth it. When I impart of myself I hope that
person deserves it. I want to mirror my own
expectations, be all that and more for this
person. I want to find that chemistry that I'm
helpless to escape. That ingrained sexual ecstasy
that cannot be explained. Then as we lay there
breathlessly in an intimate embrace I want to
communicate effortlessly, by the look etched on

my face, the extent to which my partner is able to constantly amaze me. I want it all. The good, the real, the beautiful, the love that's written in the stars. The bad, ugly, and pitiful that's bound to fall apart. I want to live through everything so I'll be ready if by chance I happen to find real love. I'll have experienced enough to recognize its veracity. So with an adamant tenacity I will continue to search for someone that loves like me. Someone that will accept 100% of who I am and love me all the more. Before senescence makes of me an eyesore I want to experience the apex of this feeling we all live for. This craving we all long for. I don't know. Maybe I'm looking for too much. If and when I find love, I want to lose it again. After I build it for years, I want it to come to an end. I want to comprehend the pain of heartbreak for myself. Be completely overwhelmed and have to bid my love farewell. I want to fall out of love so I can understand the balance. I want to suffocate in silence. Be saddened by the absence of my transient companion. And when my heart splits I want it to scar and callous. Prepare me for the challenge of granting another person access to this annex of my soul. Use that would be malice as future damage control. I want to be both emotionally vulnerable and tough. I don't know. Maybe I'm not looking for enough. Frankly, I don't give a damn. I am but a man in pursuit of something I may never fully understand. But I don't think it's something that I'm unworthy of. I know plenty of people that believe they have fallen in love. Maybe I'm just unique. Maybe the problem is that I've attempted to seek love out for so long. As if it was something that belonged to me all along. How wrong could I be? If love is somewhere out there among the facedown tarot cards of my destiny, then I must abandon this mental density that makes me think I can force it out of hiding. Throughout the years I have felt my need for love subsiding. Residing in my heart is an immense capacity for romance and the rapture that comes with it. Let me be explicit and not beat around the bush. I've tried to push myself towards love for as long as I can remember. I've surrendered myself time and again to this distempered emotion and the splendor it engenders. But all to the same end. So how can I pretend that this will be any different? In my ignorance I allowed myself to believe that I could achieve the Hollywood love that we see on the screen. So coolly depicted, this love beats all odds as if gods are the ones that have scripted the hopeless facade of this timeless mirage that becomes less and less solid the closer you get. So forget what I said. I've been misled and lied to by the aforementioned

deities. And I can see clearly that they won't
waste their time on me, so I won't waste mine
either. I'll change my procedures. I can love at
my leisure. Let come whatever may and lower
both my guard and expectations. I'll be patient
with love and in time it will come. And when it
finally does, whoever you are, I hope I am
enough. I hope you'll be willing to call my bluff
when I claim that I don't believe in love.
Because when you do I will show you just how
much I have to give. And for however much
longer I live you will be loved by someone to
the utmost extent. I will strive to deserve the
love I accept. And whatever I get I'll give back,
times ten.

Broken Eyes

The sadness in her glowing eyes
was masked by the warmth of a smile
hours rehearsed

Someone in a distant reality tells her
they're beautiful

In her mind
she responds that kaleidoscopes
appear most magnificent
when they are severely cracked

She wonders if her eyes simply reflect
a soul that is broken and tired

She wonders if the beauty in her pain
inspires others to continue as she did

And her lips form the words
"thank you"

Beautiful Society

Tell me why? Tell me why there is such high regard for a social standard of beauty? Truly, do we believe that someone's worth should be esteemed by brand of shirt or should we brandish vocal cruelties through such disrespectful slurs. Yes, sticks and stones cause bones to break, but hurtful words will cut like blades, the things we say can leave a myriad of scars and though their depths will always vary, it's very hard for them to fade. From a young age we are subjected to the world of media and posts where people boast their accolades, their wealth, and very often, too, their bodies. I find it odd we never post about our health until someone is sick, or dying, we never share that we are trying, but only say that we've succeeded. The inspiration that we've needed gets deleted, cropped, and edited, so the mainstream stays embedded with the farce of instantaneous perfection. This infection of ideals appeals to individuals as well as the collection of humanity on far more grand a scale. If you're not winning then you fail. If you're not of the 1% then you just do not fit the bill and still what's worse they make you think that they're the ones that will provide you with the things you need to fill the blanks and build a happy life. Well, guess what? They lied. They told you that your scars are unattractive, that your wrinkles have to go, that your car is underwhelming, that you need designer clothes. They said that boys have to be blah blah blah and ladies always la la la, rebuttal with a 'que sera' and a French like upturned nose, because I'm telling you they lied. You are beautiful. They will never understand the hardships you had to withstand to be where you are today. All the things you heard them say about the way they think you ought to be do not deserve a 'probably', apology, or 'maybe they were right'. They're not. For example, let's get one thing straight, stretch marks are kinda hot. But that's a matter for another time, we still have lies left to address. They'll do their best to ruin you in your own mind so they can sell you the solution, it's advertised pollution that they've bottled as perfume. You see, they want you to consume their product so they get you to assume you gotta have whatever's new and hottest all so they recoup the profit. The system is disgusting, and it's all built on a lie. How are they gonna tell you that the wrinkles 'round your eyes that come out each time you smile aren't beautiful and endearing? How are they gonna say that the freckles on your face have no place there, as if your sun kissed skin belongs to them? And honestly why should they care? How are they going to attempt to compare different types of beauties? The sun falls on the horizon in such a wide array of hues bringing immeasurable views, and the wonder that ensues is one that requires darkness. No matter how magnificent the sunset, the stars are beautiful regardless. And still there's some that disregard this and wait for dawn's first morning light. What for one does not move the core to carry balzened torch of weary soul, for another is extraordinary and inspires homage as its toll. There is beauty in most everything because the eyes that all behold are not the same in shape, color, or preference, so the notion that a reference built by stupid social standards holds the answer to what you should do to be considered beautiful is ridiculous. You are beautiful. And believe it or not we can take back control and help console the broken souls this system has left in shambles. We can actually dismantle their conduit of corporate cruelty, by reminding one another we're not so different and our beauty lies not in the lies that we've been told, and furthermore, not in the eyes that us behold, because beauty is not something that we have, or add, are defined or described by. You. ARE. Beautiful. That is 'are' as in the verb 'to be', so when I say you are beautiful it means that I believe that you are redefining beauty. Every action that you take, every word, and yes every mistake, helps you become who you are now. No wrinkle, freckle, dimple, no scar, no birth or stretch mark could ever detract from the beauty in your soul. And that, to me, is beautiful.

Innate Senescence

Flow through me, sands of time. Connect these weary joints of mine like constellations in the open heavens. Fill me with strength. Strip me of memory, of love, of pain. Weave my cycle of life in every direction like endless rows of grain that grow, wither, and sprout again to ripen in their season on a back country road. Who knows where we'll go? Like a doe in the dark you are silent but wary. Like a lost fawn in your fields, I'm alone. Hold me, dear time. Though your chalice of age may be bitter, I drink. Your love tastes warm like the sunlight that wrinkles my skin. Begin now, or before, or never, it's fine. With you I am safe. Like any attempt to quit the sweet poison inside of this stick I keep breathing, I tell myself that my needing for you is within my control. But even I don't believe me. Don't leave me. Let your roots and my own intertwine like the grandest of oaks in the mightiest woods. Your harmony, balance, and beauty complete me. Draw me in. Allow me to see your true nature. I'm willing to wager all that I have that the candor beneath your reality actually affably approaches the distinct duality of eternity itself. A divine dichotomy, hinging on

the improbably true fact that all things that exist
do so due to your presence. Make me one with
you. Give thought to my conscience with adept
incessance. Allow me to feel of your essence.
Make me infinite. Innate senescence.

Shoes

45

Walk in mine. I'd be surprised if you made it
half a mile. You see, this smile I wear bears
traces of resemblance to the laces on your
sneakers; it hides the heavy tongue of one who's
words can be used to heal or hurt but so often
chooses silence. Why is it that if someone needs
them, I'll offer shoes from off my feet in order
to relieve them, always believing they'll return
the favor and the karmic circle will be whole?
But instead, after they've tread so harshly on my
sole, they leave and my bare feet are left to bleed
and mark with red my path in search of ways to
self console.

Tornado Town

Everything's changed. It's all the same. Today we mourn the death of yesterday and in our sorrow celebrate the coming of tomorrow. We borrow a smile in an effort to hide the pain. As if to say that if the world knew we were hurt, that would somehow be worse than trying to retain this image of perfect that costs happiness, health, and drives us insane.

Nothing has changed. We're still the same. Falling in love with someone who doesn't deserve it. Convincing ourselves that it's definitely worth it when we know in the same heart that they've broken already that life was never meant to make us feel quite this heavy.

Nothing has changed. Nothing's the same. Each day we age we are one second younger as we trace our steps back to the end. We cannot comprehend the effects of limitless time when met with our infinite potential for growth. Therefore, the heights we are able to climb remain forever unknown.

Everything's changed. We're not the same. Our infinite souls cannot be contained by these frail earthly frames. We have accepted the fact that ours is the fate of greatness and glory. Not found in the fame of mortal significance, but rather the aim of telling our story and leaving our mark by making a difference.

Nothing has changed. We're still the same.

And before we decide to welcome the end.

We can start over again.

In Case You Didn't Know

And here you are again. Sat with your back pressed against the wall so hard you start to worry the paint will peel. I know your knees are tucked up in front of you to serve as a shield to the unknown dangers that could arise at any moment. I know you've never really spoken your truth but instead you've always chosen to pen down your worries and burn them. In that bathroom sink with the window open you let your pain go and the flames sing. I know those scars from your parents still sting and you carry the weight of them like war medals though you wish you never earned them. I know that your hands hurt when you hear a door open. I know that you're secretly hoping that no one will notice you're up here alone. I know you're still making sense of the phrase home is where the heart is, which is why you've grown to expect to be left broken-hearted by those that were supposed to help you navigate every stuttering palpitation. I know you feel emotions deeply and remember the sensation of hurt and hope and use one simultaneously to cope with the other. Hope seems scarier than hurt because it was something you'd never known. Yet your prayers were spent begging for hope because hurt is all you were ever shown. I know you've grown into a child that seeks security but will not ask for comfort. I know that you believe the hurtful words that you heard echoing from your mother. I know your father never cared, you and your siblings grew up scared, but you were always there to protect and look out for one another. I know you did your best in tests at school to spare yourself the beatings. Memorized chapters of advanced teachings to always stay one step ahead. I know your bed was wet more nights than it was dry. I know you stayed more silent than a summer breeze at nights when you would cry. I know you tried your best in sports to search for some type of recognition. I know you learned there was safety in repetition of certain behaviors and cycles. I know. Trust me. I know. You have strength that you can't see and talents you've been made to believe that you need to hide. It's no wonder you never realized all the amazing things about you. I doubt you will see it all at once, but I still want to try to show you. In case you didn't know, you are amazing. You learned young how to observe a situation and see it from more than one perspective. The shields you put up helped you become introspective and wiser than your years should have permitted. Your ears learned to listen to more than what was said, but

also what wasn't as well. In case you didn't
know, one day you will be able to sell those
words you would burn in fear they were found
by the wrong person. You will stand before
curtains and crowds and be loud in convictions.
And people will listen. In case you didn't know,
your scars are not meant to be hidden. Each one
is a reminder that you were stronger than any
attack, that you could bounce back and heal
from anything that you're faced with. So let
shame be replaced with a sense of
accomplishment. In case you didn't know, and
this might be much to your astonishment, you
are not the result of abandonment. You are not
alone. There are so many that you've been
preparing to meet that will love you, and some
of them will stay. Some of them will make sense
of the phrase that home is where the heart is.
Some of them will take hold of those pieces of
yourself that you've guarded and remind you it's
ok. Remind you that broken does not equal
bested, but rather a heart that is broken and still
beating is one that has been tested, battered,
bruised, but somehow kept on believing that
hope was out there somewhere for them to
claim. In case you didn't know, your name is
synonymous with intelligent, intuitive, creative,
outgoing, and good with words. And you will
use these gifts time and time again to provide

comfort and refuge to those who are hurt. In case you didn't know, your mother was wrong. Those words that she burned into your bones, spat out like stones to shatter the glass house you'd so carefully crafted, those same words she blasted you with everyday, those words she hung on her wall so you could see them again and again meant nothing at all. Your worth could not be determined by some other person, be they your mother or otherwise. Your worth could not be measured, represented, or compared to whatever she cared to say that you symbolize. She was wrong. In case you didn't know. It's okay to cry. It's okay to realize that other people will see that you too have emotions. Some of them will come along solely to help you expose them. Others will be there to comfort and console them. Others to teach you how to control them. In case you didn't know, you are strong enough to break the cycles. Not just your own, but some generational patterns will end with you. You have tended to others wounds for so long and neglected your own. But I am here for you. Doing what we always seem to do. But this time it's different for me and you, because I never thought I would be the one to help see me through the same situations that made you me and made me you. But we are strong enough to recognize what hurt us, face it and grow. We are present enough to take our own destiny, shape it and show anyone that has ever doubted us that we will make it and slow down for no one and nothing at all, we will not dim our shine. In case the world didn't know, it's my turn, it's our time.

She Is

She is there. In the sunlight at daybreak as the sun wakes to welcome in new possibilities and hope for the brightness we all long for in our darkest of days. She is the warmth of those rays that stretch out at dawn to reach what was once stricken in shadows. She is there in the morning dew and the song of the blue and the blackbird, as if God manufactured her soul out of rhythm, her bones out of rhyme, each line and each note of her heavenly melody sings every time that she speaks. She is there at the peak of each mountain range overlooking the valleys and alleys of each city street that make up the breathtaking view. In the rivers and creeks that glimmer on the edge of every precipice, cascading into pools of tranquil repose. She is there in each flow of a waterfall, each skip of a stone, each butterfly's wing beat, each whistling tone of nature's true beauty. She is what proves we as a species can do so much more. Never before seen and never again can the universe replicate the level to which she seems to elevate herself to. What can she be compared to? The sun? But she does not burn as harshly, nor does she shine her light where it does not deserve to be. Brilliance of such rarity was not made to be commonplace or expected. The moon? But she waxes while waning and grows ever greater when her cycle restarts. And how could a heart such as hers ever be versed with a light that's reflected? The stars? Though with all of their might, their dazzling light could not compare to the one that she emanates. Her smile can generate warmth of its own to double as home to the downtrodden, the outcast, the forgotten and afraid. How can one woman be both softer than cotton but sharper than blade? Her eyes. Her eyes hold her strength that pours out like ocean but is sturdy as earth. Her worth cannot be measured or given value sufficient. Through any condition or struggle or fight, the only consistence is the gift of her light. A better friend you will not be able to find and that is fact indisputable. And through all this, she dares to be so effortlessly, inexplicably, and undeniably beautiful. So compare her to the sunset that holds not one single color with a hue that can outdo the view of her eyes. Compare her to the ocean whose seafoam and tide could never wish to compete with her smile. Put her against the constellations that dance through the sky, the caliginous moon that lights up the night, the sound of the earth as nature strikes any chorus, the dazzling sun through the leaves of the forest, the fields and their flowers, the snow, or the lightning, the universe and her power, both endless and frightening, against waterfalls, sunrise, rainbows, birds, and butterflies. Combine all the above. Rest assured, without doubt, their beauty would not be as deep as, the stretch of their warmth could not match her reaches, and my fervent belief is, they would not be quite nearly as stunning as she is.

The Gist Of It

Humanity is defined as "all human beings collectively; the human race." Humanity is defined as "the quality of being humane; kindness; benevolence; goodwill." We are not perfect, and still, there is good to be found in every one of us. That person right in front of us is composed of the same flesh and bone that our own bodies house. We all arrive into this world in a very similar state. Innocent. Loud. Beautiful. And though we all grow in unique and individual ways, each of us stays beautiful. In appearance as well as in heart. We are divine works of art that double as sentient entities, complex identities that have the propensity to boast our own density and downplay so often the utter immensity of our amazing potential. Humanities is defined as "literature, language, philosophy, art, etc." So no matter the dialect or debate, by sweat of the brow or by fate, we are human. We are art. We are a spark set ablaze in poetry. We are life born into culture, we are culture birthed by our breath. We are passion and depth, we are more than mere mortals here waiting for death. We are the meeting ground and matrimony between all dichotomies. We are

where good meets evil, and laughter meets grief,
where darkness finds light, where wrongs learn
their rights. We are the prodigy offspring of
chaos and peace. We are the twinkling ambience
between sunshine and moonlight where dusk's
golden hue turns silver and blue to make way for
the nighttime. We are lifelines of love, harborers
of hope who fight on and cope with what once
might have broke us. We are strength of the soul,
windows to worlds without end. Energy high
and entropy low, we flow with the will of
alignment, vibrant and ever increasing in
brightness. Inside us resides the awe striking
likeness of potential that knows no bounds.
Wherever we're found, know the good times
will roll. Know that we'll take our toll, leave our
mark, light our spark and inspire the fire that
will burn away chains they have tethered, light
us through storms we have weathered, and warm
us to the core of our hearts and our homes. We
are poetry in motion, writing lines with each step
in our lifetime of poems. We will go through the
thick of it, we will unlock the limitless, uplift the
spiritless, push past the little shit. We are human.
We are art. We are infinite. And that's just the
gist of it.